U.S. Sites and Symbols

★★★★★★★★★★★★

Birds

Leia Tait

WEIGL PUBLISHERS INC.

Published by Weigl Publishers Inc.
350 5th Avenue, Suite 3304, PMB 6G
New York, NY 10118-0069

Website: www.weigl.com

Library of Congress Cataloging-in-Publication Data

Tait, Leia.
 Birds/ Leia Tait.
           p. cm. –(U.S. Sites and symbols)
 Includes index.
 ISBN: 978-1-59036-891-6 (soft cover: alk. Paper)—ISBN: 978-1-59036-890-9 (hard cover: alk. Paper) 1. State birds—United States—Juvenile literature. 2. State birds—United States—Pictorial works—Juvenile literature. I. Title.
 QL682.T35 2009
 598.0973—dc22

 2008015824

Editor: Danielle LeClair
Designer: Kathryn Livingstone

Photograph Credits

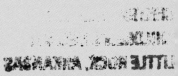

Contents

What are Symbols?

A symbol is an item that stands for something else. Objects, artworks, or living things can all be symbols. Every U.S. state has official symbols, or emblems. These items represent the people, history, and culture of the state. State symbols create feelings of pride and citizenship among the people who live there. Each of the 50 states has an official bird symbol. It is called the state bird.

State Bird History

People have been using bird symbols for thousands of years. They are the most common animal emblems in the world. In the early 1900s, many U.S. states began adopting official flowers. Women's clubs, bird lovers, and schoolchildren urged state governments to choose official birds as well. In the 1920s, the idea of state bird emblems was promoted by Mrs. Katherine B. Tipperrs of the General Federation of Women's Clubs in Washington, DC. Mrs. Tipperrs asked women's groups to hold public votes in states without an official bird. As a result, many states chose their official bird during the 1920s and 1930s.

In many states, women's clubs started the process of choosing an official bird.

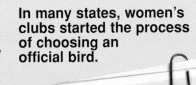

Finding State Birds by Region

Alaska

Hawai'i

Washington

Montana

Oregon

Idaho

Wyoming

The West

Nevada

Utah

Colorado

California

Arizona

New Mexico

Each state has a bird symbol. In this book, the states are organized by region. These regions are the West, the Midwest, the South, and the Northeast. Each region is unique because of its land, people, and wildlife. Throughout this book, the regions are color coded. To find a state bird, first find the state using the map on this page. Then, turn to the pages that are the same color as that state.

North Dakota
Minnesota
South Dakota
Wisconsin
Michigan
Iowa
Nebraska
Illinois
Indiana
Ohio
Kansas
Missouri
Kentucky
West Virginia
Virginia
New York
Pennsylvania
New Hampshire
Vermont
Maine
Massachusetts
Rhode Island
Connecticut
New Jersey
Delaware
Maryland
North Carolina
Tennessee
Oklahoma
Arkansas
South Carolina
Georgia
Texas
Alabama
Mississippi
Louisiana
Florida

The Northeast

The Midwest

The South

Web Crawler

Find out facts about each state at **www.americaslibrary.gov**. Click on "Explore the States."

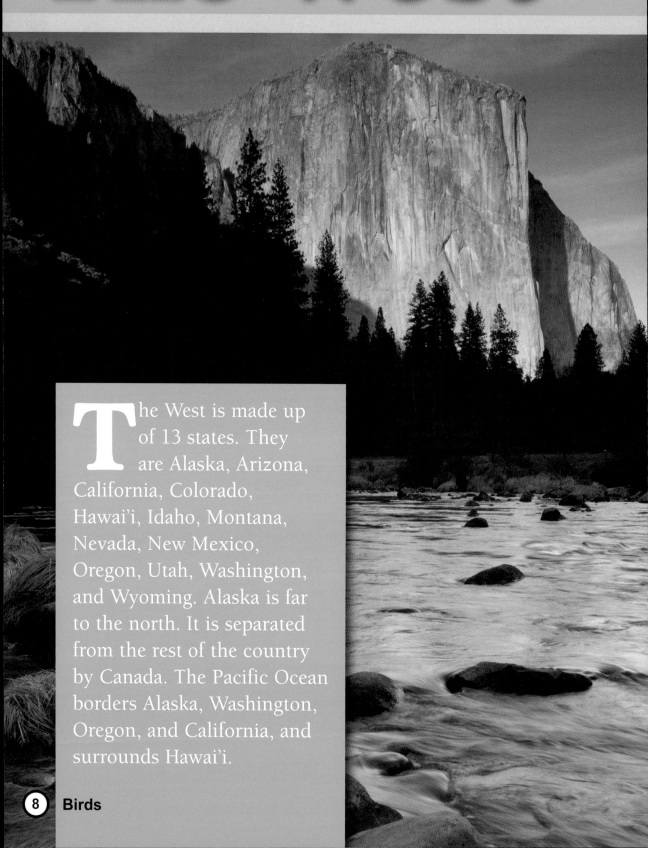

The West

The West is made up of 13 states. They are Alaska, Arizona, California, Colorado, Hawai'i, Idaho, Montana, Nevada, New Mexico, Oregon, Utah, Washington, and Wyoming. Alaska is far to the north. It is separated from the rest of the country by Canada. The Pacific Ocean borders Alaska, Washington, Oregon, and California, and surrounds Hawai'i.

Colorado

Arizona

Hawai'i

Alaska

California

The West has many different landforms. There are glaciers in Alaska and volcanoes on Hawai'i. Giant redwood forests grow in Oregon. Deserts cover parts of Arizona, California, Nevada, and Utah. The Rocky Mountains run through Alaska, Washington, Idaho, Montana, Wyoming, Utah, Colorado, and New Mexico.

About 65 million people live in the West. American Indians, Asians, Hispanics, and people of British and German backgrounds make up the largest cultural groups. Nearly four million people live in Los Angeles, California. It is the region's largest city.

Web Crawler

Trace important events in the history of the West at **www.pbs.org/ weta/thewest/events**.

Discover the West's natural wonders by clicking on the states at **www.nps.gov**.

Alaska
Willow Ptarmigan

Alaska's state bird is the willow ptarmigan. It was chosen in 1955. The willow ptarmigan is a chicken-like bird with short, rounded wings. In summer, its feathers are chestnut brown. In winter, they become white. This helps the bird **camouflage** in nature.

Arizona
Cactus Wren

The cactus wren has been Arizona's state bird since 1931. This bird is brown with a white stripe over each of its eyes. It uses its long, curved beak to hunt for insects on the ground and under shrubs. The cactus wren lives in the deserts of the West. It builds its nest in tall cacti. The cactus wren is known for its noisy "cha cha cha cha cha" song.

California
California Quail

The California quail became the California state bird in 1931. This small, plump bird is about 10 inches long. It has a short black beak and a curved black plume on its forehead. The plume is made of six overlapping feathers. It is larger on males than females. In nature, the California quail lives in grasslands and **chaparrals**. It is also found in parks and other places near people.

Colorado
Lark Bunting

Colorado's state bird is the lark bunting. It was chosen in 1931. The lark bunting is a type of sparrow. It lives in prairie grassland throughout North America. Lark buntings are mostly brown with a streaked chest. In spring, males change to black with a white patch on their wings. Lark buntings are known for their song. It is a complicated mix of whistles, trills, and rattles.

Hawai'i
Nene

In 1957, Hawai'i made the nene its state bird. The nene is a type of goose. It lives on grassy slopes created by lava flows from Hawai'i's volcanoes. The nene has a black head, bill, legs, and feet. Diagonal rows of white feathers grow on its neck. The nene is **endangered**. It is illegal to hunt this bird.

Idaho
Mountain Bluebird & Peregrine Falcon

Idaho has two official bird symbols. Its state bird is the mountain bluebird. It was chosen in 1931. Mountain bluebird males are bright sky-blue. Females are gray with blue wings and tails. Idaho is the only state to have an official state **raptor**. This is the peregrine falcon. This bird is one of the fastest animals on Earth. It can reach speeds of 200 miles per hour.

Montana
Western Meadowlark

The western meadowlark was chosen as Montana's state bird in 1931. It has black stripes on its head, wings, and back. Its chest is bright yellow with a black "V." The western meadowlark is one of the most popular state symbols. It is the official bird of five other states. They are Kansas, Nebraska, North Dakota, Oregon, and Wyoming.

Nevada
Mountain Bluebird

Nevada has the same state bird as Idaho. The mountain bluebird became the state's official bird in 1967. Mountain bluebirds live in the mountains and grasslands of western North America. They are migratory. This means they move with the seasons. Mountain bluebirds often travel in flocks of up to 50 birds.

New Mexico
Chaparral Bird

The chaparral bird became New Mexico's state bird in 1949. This is a type of cuckoo bird. It lives in the desert. Chaparral birds are also called roadrunners. They can run as fast as 20 miles per hour.

Oregon
Western Meadowlark

In 1927, Oregon schoolchildren chose the western meadowlark as the state bird. The western meadowlark is a songbird. Its flute-like song has 7 to 10 notes.

Utah
California Gull

Utah's state bird is the California gull. It has been important to people in Utah since 1848. That year, swarms of crickets attacked the state's crops. Flocks of California gulls saved the crops by eating the crickets. The California gull became the state bird in 1955.

Washington
American Goldfinch

The American goldfinch became Washington's state bird in 1951. This small bird is also called the willow goldfinch and the eastern goldfinch. Males have a bright yellow body with a patch of black on the head. Their wings and tail also are black. Females have an olive-yellow body with dark brown wings and tail. The American goldfinch is also the state bird of Iowa and New Jersey.

Wyoming
Western Meadowlark

Wyoming's state bird is the western meadowlark. It was chosen in 1927. Western meadowlarks build their nests on the ground. They search the ground with their beak to find food. Western meadowlarks eat seeds, snails, and insects, such as beetles, cutworms, spiders, caterpillars, grasshoppers.

The Midwest

The Midwest is in the center of the United States. It lies between the Rocky Mountains in the west and the Appalachian Mountains in the northeast. The Ohio River separates the Midwest from the South. Canada lies to the north. There are 12 states in the Midwest. They are Illinois, Indiana, Iowa, Kansas, Michigan, Minnesota, Missouri, Nebraska, North Dakota, Ohio, South Dakota, and Wisconsin.

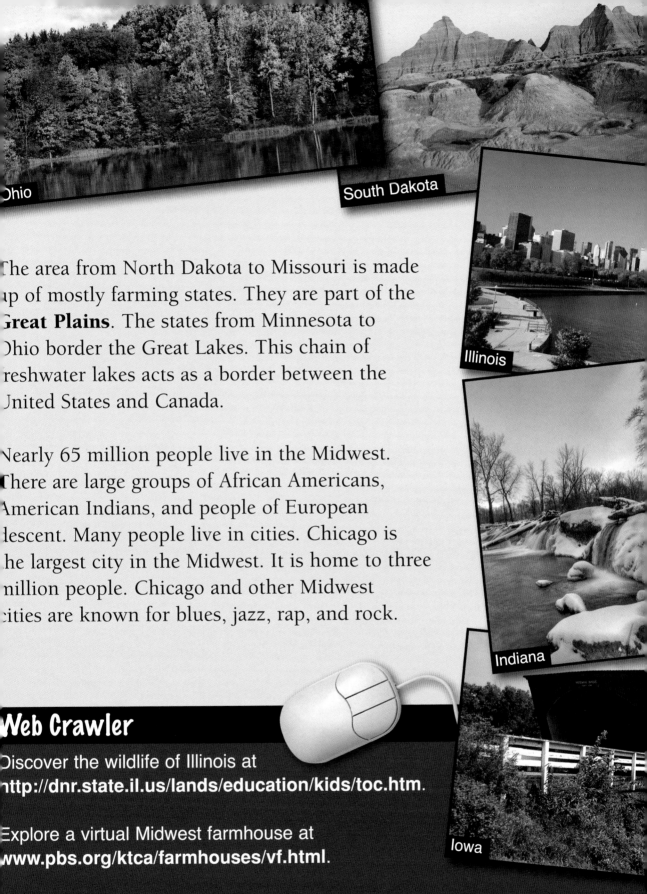

Ohio

South Dakota

Illinois

The area from North Dakota to Missouri is made up of mostly farming states. They are part of the **Great Plains**. The states from Minnesota to Ohio border the Great Lakes. This chain of freshwater lakes acts as a border between the United States and Canada.

Nearly 65 million people live in the Midwest. There are large groups of African Americans, American Indians, and people of European descent. Many people live in cities. Chicago is the largest city in the Midwest. It is home to three million people. Chicago and other Midwest cities are known for blues, jazz, rap, and rock.

Indiana

Web Crawler

Discover the wildlife of Illinois at
http://dnr.state.il.us/lands/education/kids/toc.htm.

Explore a virtual Midwest farmhouse at
www.pbs.org/ktca/farmhouses/vf.html.

Iowa

Illinois
Cardinal

The Illinois state bird is the cardinal. It was chosen in 1929. The cardinal is the most popular bird emblem in the United States. Along with Illinois, it is the state bird of Indiana, Kentucky, Ohio, North Carolina, Virginia, and West Virginia. Male cardinals are bright red with a black face.

Indiana
Cardinal

In 1933, Indiana chose the cardinal for its state bird. Like many bird **species**, female cardinals look different from males. Female cardinals are tan. They

have patches of red on their head, wings, tail, and breast. A female's coloring helps camouflage her when she sits on the nest.

Iowa
American Goldfinch

Iowa's state bird is the American goldfinch. It was chosen in 1933. The American goldfinch lives in weedy fields, orchards, and gardens. Its long legs and claws help it perch on plants. Iowa and New Jersey also share this state bird.

Kansas
Western Meadowlark

Kansas' state bird is the western meadowlark. The Kansas government chose this bird as an emblem in 1937. The yellow and brown colors of the western meadowlark match the colors of Kansas's state flower, the sunflower.

Michigan
American Robin

The American robin became Michigan's state bird in 1931. It is also called the robin redbreast. The American robin has a dark gray head, back, and wings. Its chest is an orange-red color. It is one of the best-known birds in North America. It is also the state bird of Connecticut and Wisconsin.

Minnesota
Common Loon

Minnesota chose the common loon as its state bird in 1961. These water birds are known for their four

unique calls. The tremolo sounds like a crazy laugh. It can be used in greeting or to express worry. Mates use a soft wail to locate each other in the water. The yodel is a long, rising call that males use to defend their space. Family members use a soft hoot to find each other.

Missouri
Eastern Bluebird
& Bobwhite Quail

Missouri chose the eastern bluebird as its state bird in 1927. The bird's head, back, and wings are bright blue. Its chest is red-orange, and its belly is white. Eastern bluebirds live east of the Rocky Mountains. Missouri also has a state **game** bird. It is a chicken-like bird called the bobwhite quail. It was chosen in 2007.

Nebraska
Western Meadowlark

In the 1920s, bird lovers, schoolchildren, and women's groups in Nebraska voted the western meadowlark their choice for state bird. In 1929, the state government made it official. Western meadowlarks are known for their joyous song. Males will sing to claim a space as their own. They often perch on fence posts while singing.

North Dakota
Western Meadowlark

North Dakota's state bird is the western meadowlark. The state government adopted this bird in 1947. Western meadowlarks build their nests on the ground, most often in grassy fields. Their nests are dome-shaped, with a side tunnel entrance. They are woven from grass, pine needles, and horsehair.

Ohio
Cardinal

The cardinal is the state bird of Ohio. Ohio chose the cardinal as its state bird in 1933. Cardinals are found in all of Ohio's 88 counties. The bird's bright red feathers match the color of the state's official flower, the scarlet carnation.

South Dakota
Ring-Necked Pheasant

In 1943, South Dakota chose the ring-neck pheasant as its state bird. This is a chicken-like game bird from

China. Farmers first brought it to the United States in 1892, and to South Dakota in 1908. Males have a shiny green head, red face, and copper chest. They are named for the white ring around their neck. Females are spotted brown and white.

Wisconsin
American Robin

Chosen in 1949, Wisconsin's state bird is the American robin. The robin is also the state bird of Connecticut and Michigan. American robins live in forests, woodlands, and fields, as well as gardens and yards. Robins eat earthworms in the morning and berries later in day.

The South

The South is made up of 16 states. They are Alabama, Arkansas, Delaware, Florida, Georgia, Kentucky, Louisiana, Maryland, Mississippi, North Carolina, Oklahoma, South Carolina, Tennessee, Texas, Virginia, and West Virginia. The Atlantic Ocean borders the South from Delaware to the tip of Florida. A part of the Atlantic Ocean called the Gulf of Mexico stretches from Florida's west coast to Texas. Mexico lies to the south.

Florida

Alabama

Texas

The South is known for its warm weather. It also has plenty of rain. This makes it easy for plants to grow. In the past, cotton, tobacco, rice, and sugarcane were important crops in the South. They shaped southern history.

More than 100 million people live in the South. About 20 million are African American. Many people of Hispanic and European backgrounds also live there. Together, southerners share a special history and culture. Blues, gospel, rock, and country music all began in the South. Many well-known writers, such as Tennessee Williams, have lived there. The South is also known for its barbeque, Tex-Mex, and Cajun cooking.

West Virginia

Web Crawler

Read about the history of the South at **www.factmonster.com/ipka/A0875011.html**.

Explore the fun facts about the Southern states at **www.emints.org/ethemes/resources/S00000575.shtml**.

Mississippi

Alabama
Yellowhammer & Wild Turkey

Alabama's state bird is the yellowhammer, or northern flicker. It was chosen in 1927. This woodpecker is gray with yellow feathers on its wings and tail and a red mark on its neck. Alabama's state game bird is the wild turkey.

Arkansas
Mockingbird

Arkansas chose the mockingbird for its state bird in 1929. The mockingbird is mostly gray, with a white chest and belly. It has large white patches on its wings that show when the mockingbird flies.

Delaware
Blue Hen Chicken

Delaware chose the blue hen chicken as the state bird in 1939. Blue hen chickens became a symbol of Delaware during the **American Revolutionary War**.

Florida
Mockingbird

Florida's state bird is the mockingbird. It was chosen in 1927. The mockingbird can copy the songs of many other birds. Some mockingbirds can sing the songs of more than 20 different birds in 10 minutes.

Georgia
Brown Thrasher & Bobwhite Quail

Georgia chose two official birds in 1970. The brown thrasher is Georgia's state bird. It is a rust-colored songbird with a long tail. Georgia's official game bird is the bobwhite quail. These birds live in groups, called coveys, of more than 100 birds.

Kentucky
Cardinal

The cardinal became Kentucky's state bird in 1926. This bird is found in almost every state east of the Rocky Mountains. It lives in meadows and forests, as well as in city gardens and parks.

Louisiana
Brown Pelican

Louisiana's state bird is the brown pelican. This is a large sea bird that lives on U.S. coasts. It is about 4 feet long and has a white and yellow head and brown body. Louisiana is known as "the pelican state." The pelican appears on the state seal and the state flag.

Maryland
Baltimore Oriole

In 1947, the Baltimore oriole became Maryland's state bird. This songbird is known for its colorful feathers. Males have a bright orange chest and belly, a black head and back, and black wings with white stripes. Females are yellow-orange with gray wing stripes.

Mississippi
Mockingbird & Wood Duck

Mississippi has two bird emblems. The state bird is the mockingbird. It was chosen in 1927. Mississippi also has an official state **waterfowl**. This is the wood duck. It was chosen in 1974.

North Carolina
Cardinal

North Carolina's state bird is the cardinal. It was chosen in 1943. Cardinals eat seeds, grains, fruit, and insects. They will often snack from backyard birdfeeders. With a healthy diet, most cardinals can live about 15 years.

Oklahoma
Scissor-tailed Flycatcher & Wild Turkey

Oklahoma's state bird is the scissor-tailed flycatcher. This is a gray songbird with an orange-pink underside. Its long, forked tail looks like a pair of scissors. The scissor-tailed flycatcher became Oklahoma's state bird in 1951. In 1990, the state also chose an official game bird. This is the wild turkey. It lives in forests and marshlands throughout the eastern United States.

South Carolina
Carolina Wren & Wild Turkey

South Carolina first chose the mockingbird as its state bird. However, in 1948, the people of South Carolina voted again and chose the Carolina wren. Carolina wrens are small reddish-brown songbirds. They sing loudly and often. Males may

sing up to 3,000 times a day. South Carolina also has an official wild game bird. The wild turkey was chosen for this emblem in 1976.

Tennessee
Mockingbird & Bobwhite Quail

Tennessee has both a state bird and a state game bird. The mockingbird is Tennessee's state bird. It was chosen in 1933. Mockingbirds are common throughout the South. Tennessee's state game bird is the bobwhite quail. This bird is named for the sound of the male's loud call, "bob-bob white."

Texas
Mockingbird

Like Arkansas, Florida, Mississippi, and Tennessee, Texas' state bird is the mockingbird. It was chosen in 1927. Mockingbirds sing long, complicated songs. In spring and summer, male mockingbirds will sing all day and night.

Virginia
Cardinal

The cardinal became Virginia's state bird in 1950. Cardinals travel very little. Most live their entire lives within a mile of where they were born. They build bowl-shaped nests in bushes and small trees.

West Virginia
Cardinal

Like Virginia, West Virginia's state bird is the cardinal. It was chosen in 1949. Cardinals are special birds because females sing as well as males. From their nest, a female cardinal will call to her mate in song.

The Northeast

The Northeast is the smallest region in the United States. It is east of the Great Lakes and south of Canada. The Atlantic Ocean borders the Northeast coast. There are nine states in the Northeast. They are Connecticut, Maine, Massachusetts, New Hampshire, New Jersey, New York, Pennsylvania, Rhode Island, and Vermont.

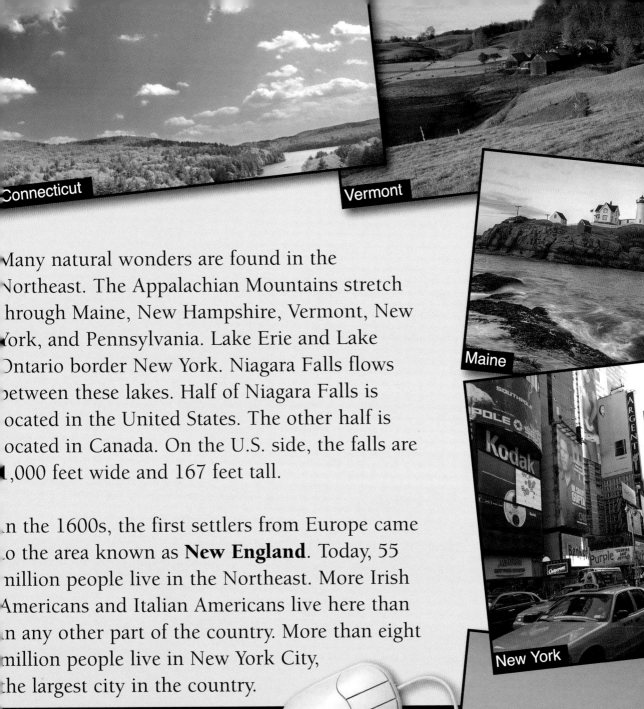

Connecticut

Vermont

Maine

New York

Pennsylvania

Many natural wonders are found in the Northeast. The Appalachian Mountains stretch through Maine, New Hampshire, Vermont, New York, and Pennsylvania. Lake Erie and Lake Ontario border New York. Niagara Falls flows between these lakes. Half of Niagara Falls is located in the United States. The other half is located in Canada. On the U.S. side, the falls are 1,000 feet wide and 167 feet tall.

In the 1600s, the first settlers from Europe came to the area known as **New England**. Today, 55 million people live in the Northeast. More Irish Americans and Italian Americans live here than in any other part of the country. More than eight million people live in New York City, the largest city in the country.

Web Crawler

Learn more about New England at **www.discovernewengland.org**.

See spectacular views of Niagara Falls at **www.niagarafallsstatepark.com/Destination_PhotoGallery.aspx**.

Connecticut
American Robin

Like Michigan and Wisconsin, Connecticut's state bird is the American robin. It was chosen in 1943. American robins are named after a red-breasted bird found in England, but the two are not related. American robins sing a cheery-sounding song. Their eggs are a pale blue color, known as robin's egg blue.

Maine
Black-Capped Chickadee

Maine chose its state bird in 1927. It is the black-capped chickadee. This plump, round songbird has white cheeks. The top of its head and its chin are black. Its wings are gray-green. The black-capped chickadee is one of the best-loved birds in North America. It is also the state bird of Massachusetts.

Massachusetts
Black-Capped Chickadee & Wild Turkey

Massachusetts' state bird is the black-capped chickadee. It was chosen in 1941. Black-capped chickadees eat insects, spiders, seeds, and berries. They hide bits of food to eat later. One chickadee can remember thousands of different hiding spots. Massachusetts' state game bird is the wild turkey.

New Hampshire
Purple Finch

The purple finch became New Hampshire's state bird in 1957. This bird usually lives in **coniferous** forests. It eats flower buds, blossoms, nectar, fruit, and seeds. Purple finch males are reddish-purple. Females have brown and white stripes.

New Jersey
American Goldfinch

The state bird of New Jersey is the American goldfinch. New Jersey shares this emblem with Iowa and Washington. Goldfinches are social. They prefer to live in groups. In flight, goldfinches can appear as if they are dancing. They flap their wings a few times to lift up in the air. Then, they float for a few moments on closed wings.

New York
Eastern Bluebird

In 1928, New York's women chose the eastern bluebird to be the state bird. The New York government finally made this bird a state emblem in 1970. Eastern bluebirds are known for their many songs. They have different songs for courting a mate, protecting their space, and other activities. Their most common song is a sweet-sounding "chur lee."

Pennsylvania
Ruffed Grouse

Pennsylvania has an official state game bird instead of a state bird. This is the ruffed grouse. It was chosen in 1931. The ruffed grouse is a stocky, chicken-like bird that lives in Pennsylvania's forests. In winter, it will sleep in snowdrifts.

Rhode Island
Rhode Island Red

Rhode Island chose the Rhode Island Red chicken as its state bird in 1954. The breed was created 100 years earlier in Little Compton, Rhode Island. Today, it is the best-known chicken breed in the United States.

Vermont
Hermit Thrush

The hermit thrush became Vermont's state bird in 1941. This is a small, brown and white bird that lives in forests. It is found in every county in Vermont. The hermit thrush is known for its sweet, flute-like song.

The National Bird

National emblems are symbols that are used for the entire country. The American flag, known as the star-spangled banner, is one such symbol. Another is the bald eagle, which is the the national bird. The oak tree is the national tree. The official bird of the United States is the bald eagle.

Bald eagles are large, dark brown birds with a white head and tail. They are not actually bald, but piebald, which means "marked with white."

The bald eagle is the only eagle that is native to North America. It is a symbol of American strength, courage, freedom, and **immortality**.

The bald eagle appears on the Great Seal, the President's flag, and the $1 bill. It is an important image in American art, buildings, songs, and stories.

History of the Eagle

In 1782, the eagle was chosen as the American National Bird. The Founding Fathers wanted to choose an animal that was unique to the United States. At first, the golden eagle was drawn on the national seal, but since it lives in both Europe and America, the American bald eagle was used instead. President John F. Kennedy said, "the fierce beauty and proud independence of this great bird aptly symbolizes the strength and freedom of America."

Guide to State Birds

THE NATIONAL BIRD
bald eagle

ALABAMA
yellowhammer;
wild turkey

ALASKA
willow
ptarmigan

ARIZONA
mockingbird

ARKANSAS
cactus wren

CALIFORNIA
California quail

COLORADO
lark bunting

CONNECTICUT
American robin

DELAWARE
blue hen
chicken

FLORIDA
mockingbird

GEORGIA
brown
thrasher;
bobwhite quail

HAWAI'I
nene

IDAHO
mountain
bluebird;
peregrine falcon

ILLINOIS
cardinal

INDIANA
cardinal

IOWA
American
goldfinch

KANSAS
western
meadowlark

KENTUCKY
cardinal

LOUISIANA
brown pelican

MAINE
black-capped
chickadee

MARYLAND
Baltimore oriole

| **MASSACHUSETTS** black-capped chickadee; wild turkey | **MICHIGAN** American robin | **MINNESOTA** common loon | **MISSISSIPPI** mockingbird; wood duck | **MISSOURI** eastern bluebird; bobwhite quail | **MONTANA** western meadowlark |

| **NEBRASKA** western meadowlark | **NEVADA** mountain bluebird | **NEW HAMPSHIRE** purple finch | **NEW JERSEY** common American goldfinch | **NEW MEXICO** chaparral bird | **NEW YORK** eastern bluebird |

| **NORTH CAROLINA** cardinal | **NORTH DAKOTA** western meadowlark | **OHIO** cardinal | **OKLAHOMA** scissor-tailed flycatcher; wild turkey | **OREGON** western meadowlark | **PENNSYLVANIA** ruffed grouse |

| **RHODE ISLAND** Rhode Island red | **SOUTH CAROLINA** Carolina wren; wild turkey | **SOUTH DAKOTA** ring-necked pheasant | **TENNESSEE** mockingbird; bobwhite quail | **TEXAS** mockingbird | **UTAH** California gull |

| **VERMONT** hermit thrush | **VIRGINIA** cardinal | **WASHINGTON** American goldfinch | **WEST VIRGINIA** cardinal | **WISCONSIN** American robin | **WYOMING** western meadowlark |

Parts of the Bird

Birds are animals with feathers. They have two wings, two legs, a beak, and lay eggs. There are more than 9,000 species of birds on Earth. They live in all parts of the world, including deserts, rain forests, and arctic tundras. All birds share the same basic features.

WINGS All birds have wings, but not all birds fly. Flying birds use powerful muscles to flap their wings. Their wings are longer than those of birds that do not fly. Flightless birds use their wings for other activities. Penguins, for example, use their wings as paddles underwater.

BEAK Birds have beaks instead of jaws and teeth. Beaks have various shapes for different uses. Sharp, curved beaks are used to tear meat. Cone-shaped beaks are used to crack seeds. All birds use their beaks to preen, or comb, their feathers. This helps keep their feathers in place and working well.

FEATHERS

Birds are the only animals with feathers. Soft down feathers close to the skin help birds keep warm. Contour feathers cover most of a bird's body. They streamline the bird and help it fly. They are often waterproof. A male's contour feathers are often bright and colorful. This helps attract mates. Natural-colored feathers help both males and females blend in to their surroundings.

FEET A bird's feet are specialized depending on where it lives and what it eats. Flying birds have strong feet that help them leap into the air. Birds that live near water have webbed, paddle-like feet that help them swim. Some birds have sharp, clawed feet that help them grasp **prey**. Many flightless birds, such as the ostrich, have feet that are built for running at high speeds.

Test Your Knowledge

1 The tremolo is a type of call made by which state bird?

2 Which two states have a chicken as their state bird?

3 Which five states in the West adopted their state birds in 1931?

4 Which state bird lives on grassy slopes created by lava flows?
   a. the ring-necked pheasant (South Dakota)
   b. the nene (Hawai'i)
   c. the willow ptarmigan (Alaska)
   d. the hermit thrush (Vermont)

5 How many states have the cardinal as their official state bird?

6 How many states have an official game bird?

7 Which state is known as "the pelican state"?
   a. Baltimore
   b. Utah
   c. New Hamphire
   d. Louisiana

8 What is the national bird?

9 Which bird is the most popular state bird in the South?
- a. cardinal
- b. black-capped chicadee
- c. American robin
- d. mockingbird
- e. chaparral bird

10 The American goldfinch is the state bird of which three states?

11 Which white-cheeked bird is the state bird of Massachusetts and Maine ?
- a. eastern bluebird
- b. black-capped chicakadee
- c. bald eagle
- d. bobwhite quail
- e. cardinal

12 Which four states have a type of bluebird as their state bird?

13 The American robin is the state bird of which three states?

14 Which state bird is shared by Kansas, Montana, Nebraska, North Dakota, Oregon, and Wyoming?

15 Which state bird can run at speeds of up to 20 miles per hour?

Answers:
1. the loon—Minnesota
2. Delaware, Rhode Island
3. Arizona, California, Colorado, Idaho, and Montana
4. b. Hawai'i
5. seven—Illinois, Indiana, Kentucky, Ohio, North Carolina, Virginia, and West Virginia
6. eight—Alabama, Georgia, Massachusetts, Missouri, Oklahoma, Pennsylvania, South Carolina, Tennessee
7. d. Louisiana
8. bald eagle
9. d. mockingbird
10. Iowa, New Jersey, and Washington
11. b. black-capped chickadee
12. Idaho, Missouri, Nevada, New York
13. Connecticut, Michigan, and Wisconsin
14. the western meadowlark
15. New Mexico's chaparral bird

Create Your Own Bird Emblem

Create a bird symbol to represent you. Begin by thinking about what type of bird you want. Use this book to help you. What kinds of birds live near you? Do you prefer birds that live on the ground, in water, or in trees?

Think about how you want your bird to look. Will it have large wings for flying, or short wings and webbed feet for swimming? Will it eat meat or plants? How will its beak be shaped? What color will its feathers be? Look at the pictures in this book for help. You also can view hundreds of bird images online at **www.birdphotography.com**.

Draw your bird on a piece of paper. Use the diagram on pages 42 and 43 to help you design the parts of your bird. Color your drawing with felt markers. When you are finished, label the parts of your bird.

Write a description of your bird. What kind of bird is it? Where does it live? What does it symbolize about you?

Further Research

Many books and websites provide information on state flowers. To learn more about flowers, borrow books from the library, or surf the Internet.

Books

Most libraries have computers that connect to a database for researching information. If you input a key word, you will be provided with a list of books in the library that contain information on that topic. Non-fiction books are arranged numerically, using their call number. Fiction books are organized alphabetically by the author's last name.

Websites

Learn all you need to know about birds at **www.enchantedlearning.com/subjects/birds**. Use the menu on the left to check out different topics.

Hear thousands of different bird songs at **www.learnbirdsongs.com**.

Read more about the regions of the United States at **www.factmonster.com/ipka/A0770177.html**.

Play online bird games and activities at **www.mrnussbaum.com/birdactivities.htm**.

Glossary

American Revolutionary War: a war fought from 1775 to 1783, in which the American colonies won independence from Great Britain

camouflage: to hide by blending in with the environment

chaparrals: areas with short, shrubby plants that have dry hot summers and wet winters

coniferous: cone-bearing plants, such as firs and pines

endangered: at risk of dying out

game: animals hunted for sport

Great Plains: a vast grassland region covering 10 U.S. states and 4 Canadian provinces; used for farming and raising cattle

immortality: the state of living forever

New England: the most northeastern U.S. states—Connecticut, Rhode Island, Massachusetts, New Hampshire, Vermont, and Maine

prey: animals hunted by other animals for food

raptor: a meat-eating bird that hunts animals for food

species: groups of plants or animals that have many of the same features

waterfowl: a bird that is found in or near water

Index